I0163652

Green Thumb Gardening

Make Your Home Garden Thrive

Charlie Tucker

Charlie Tucker

Contents

Introduction

I want to thank you and congratulate you for downloading the book, *Green Thumb Gardening – Make Your Home Garden Thrive*.

I grew up watching my family spend hour after hour outside in our garden. I remember being able to walk through each row, picking the ripest fruits and vegetables and eating them right there. Nothing is more satisfying. As I grew older, I began to spend time working in the garden myself, learning all the ins and outs of the growing process.

Starting and maintaining a successful garden can be very challenging and time consuming. There are so many different choices you need to make and for each one, there are countless different methods to pick from. For new and veteran gardeners, this can become very confusing. My ultimate goal in writing this book is to make the whole process, from start to finish, much easier for anyone, no matter their experience level.

In this book, I will teach you everything there is to know about growing a home garden from the initial planning stages all the way to the final harvest. This will include germinating and planting seeds, soil compositions and maintenance, plant nutrients, and much more!

Chapter 1: Planning Your Garden

Many people decide they want to start a garden and quickly jump right into it without taking the time to plan it all out. It is important for you to plan out your garden if you want it to be successful. You need to know what you are going to plant, how you are going to plant it, and where you are going to plant it.

You also need to consider what plants you are going to place in which areas. This is because some plants can be planted together whereas others should be kept far apart. You also need to do some planning when it comes to pests, parasites, and other creatures.

The planning stage is where you will decide how you are going to keep the pests away. If you are going to use pesticides, you need to understand how they are going to affect your plants but there is another option. There are specific plants that you can place in and around your garden that will help to keep the pests and the bugs away.

Planning is also important when it comes to the placement of your garden because you do not want to hit power or phone lines when you are tilling. You also want to make sure you are aware of where the water lines are as well. Not knowing even one of these details could end up costing you a lot more than money in the long run.

To plan out your garden, you need to begin by calling the power and water companies to make sure all of the lines are marked. The next thing you will need to do is gather a tape measure and graph paper.

Once you have your tape measure and graph paper, you will begin by measuring out the space you have for your garden. Using your graph paper, draw a map of your garden, using 1 square per 6 inches, ensuring that you do not forget any permanent fixtures such as trees or ponds.

Your next step will be to plan out your paths, beds, and any other features you would like in your garden. These will be placed on your garden map. If you are going to plant flowers around your garden to ward off certain critters, you will map this as well.

Once this is done, you can begin planning the types of plants you will be planting in your garden. It is important to know what you are planting in your garden because there are companion plants that should be planted together and plants that should be kept apart.

If you are planning beans, it is a good idea to plant them with or near celery, corn, radish, cucumbers, or strawberries. On the other hand, you want to keep them away from garlic and onions. You do not want to plant beets, cabbage, Brussel sprouts, kale, or broccoli near pole beans because although these plants will not affect the beans, the beans will affect these plants.

Beets thrive best when planted with cabbage, kale, garlic, onions, broccoli, bush beans, and lettuce. Cabbage, broccoli, Brussel sprouts, and kale grow best when planted around beets, dill, onions, lettuce, potatoes, Swiss chard, spinach, and celery.

Carrots grow best with beans and tomatoes and have no adverse effect on any other plants. Celery grows best when planted near or with beans, cabbage, and tomatoes. Celery has no adverse effect on any other plants.

Corn should not be grown with tomatoes, but does well near or with melons, peas, pumpkin, cucumber, beans, and peas. Cucumber has no adverse effect on any plants, but does well when grown with cabbage, corn, peas, and beans. Eggplant has no adverse effect on any other plant, but does best when it is grown with peppers or beans.

Melons have no adverse effect on any plant, but grow best when planted with or near radish, pumpkin, squash, or corn. Onions should not be grown with any beans or any peas, however, they do well when grown with Swiss chard, lettuce, carrots, beets, and peppers.

Peas should not be grown near or with garlic or onions, but thrive when they are grown with cucumbers, beans, corn, carrots, turnip, carrots, and radish. Potatoes should never be grown with tomatoes, but do well when they are grown near or with peas, beans, or corn.

Squash does not have any adverse effect on any plants, but they do best when planted near or with pumpkins, corn, or melons.

Tomatoes should never be grown with kohlrabi, potatoes, or corn, but do well when they are planted near or with onions, cucumbers, celery, peppers, or carrots.

Pests, Bugs, and Predators:

Marigolds are great to plant in your garden, especially around your tomatoes, to ensure that there are no hornworms in your garden. You can plant marigolds throughout your garden to repel insects and other worms.

Although herbs are great food, they can also help to keep insects out of your garden. Rosemary deters beetles and can be planted around beans. Thyme should be planted near cabbage and other members of the cabbage family to repel worms.

Garlic and chives are great to keep aphids out of your garden. Oregano is like marigold in that it can be planted throughout your garden to keep pests away.

Plant these herbs throughout your garden freely in between plants to ensure there are no bugs, worms, or other pests in your garden without having to use pesticides. This will allow you to grow a completely organic garden.

When planning your garden as well as where you are going to grow your plants, and the plants that you are going to grow, you want to take the soil type, climate, and the available shade into consideration as well.

Each plant is going to grow best in different environments. This means that although most of your plants may be perfectly fine for you to grow, you need to consider the amount of sun and shade they will need and the amount of water before you plant them. For example, you do not want to plant your watermelons in an area of your garden where they will not be shaded and you want to ensure that they are in an area that will receive a lot of water.

As you are planning out what you are going to plant, and where you are going to place them, you want to make sure that you are placing plants with similar needs together. This means all of your high water plants will be in one area while all of your low water plants will be in another. This will ensure that you are not drowning one plant while giving another the water it needs.

You also need to think about where your water is going to come from. Do you live in an area that is going to provide your plants with the water they need or are you going to have to bring the water to them? If you need to bring the water to them, how exactly are you going to do this? You see, many people do not think about this when they are planting their garden and find that they need hundreds of feet of water hose just to get water to their garden. This is something that should be planned well in advance.

Finally, you need to think about the type of garden you are going to be planting. Are you going to use raised beds? Are you going to use traditional garden rows? Maybe you want to grow a garden forest or a container garden. You may even choose to create a hanging garden! These are all types of gardens that you need to consider when you are creating your garden plan. You may choose to use several of these when you design your garden and there is no way for you to design your garden wrong as long as you focus on ensuring you place your plants in the correct areas.

Finally, you need to decide if you are going to place any fixtures in your garden. Do you want your garden to become a relaxing place that you can go spend time at when you are not working, while growing food at the same time? If so, you may decide that you want to place a bench in the middle of your garden. Another option is to place a small pond in the middle of the garden. Or you can simply choose to place no fixtures in your garden and use it for nothing more than growing your next meal.

The layout of your garden is completely up to you and it should work with your life. It should ensure that you are able to work in your garden and care for your plants in the way you want to without it seeming like a full-time job.

Chapter 2: All About Raised Beds and How to Build Boxes

Raised beds seem to be all the trend right now. They make it so much easier to garden because they raise the working surface up to a level that is much easier for you to reach. You do not have to worry about bending or getting down on your knees to work in your garden.

There are many benefits to having raised beds in your garden, but there are also some disadvantages. I want to talk about both the advantages and the disadvantages to ensure that you have all of the information you need before you decide to use raised beds.

As I already mentioned, raised beds are going to bring the working surface up higher, which is great for those who are elderly, disabled, or have a hard time getting down on the ground. You can raise these beds as high as you want, which means you decide at what level your working surface is.

The second benefit is that you will keep your roots above contaminated soil or away from soil that is simply not going to give your plants the nutrients they need. This is extremely beneficial if you live in an area where the soil is very rocky or where there is a lot of clay, which is not the ideal environment for planting a garden.

This means that you will never have to worry about improving your soil. You don't have to get tests done to ensure there are enough nutrients in the soil, but instead, you are able to bring in nutrient rich soil for your plants.

If you live in a very wet environment, this will help to ensure that your plant's roots do not become waterlogged because the raised bed is going to allow the water to drain away from the roots. The raised beds will also ensure that your soil does not get washed away when there is a lot of rain.

If the raised beds are high enough, they can help to keep animals such as rabbits away from the plants. This is very beneficial if you have cats or dogs because the raised beds will help to keep the cats out of your soil and it will help to ensure dogs do not urinate on your plants.

The raised beds are very neat. You do not have to worry about having a chaotic looking garden because the raised beds are going to keep everything neat, tidy and organized.

The downside of raised beds is that they are going to take extra materials that you would not need if you were to use traditional gardening. You will also find that you have to purchase soil to fill up your beds unless you have a lot of extra soil to fill the beds with. Of course, if you are purchasing the soil, you are going to find that it becomes very expensive if you are creating a very big garden.

You will have to make sure that your plants are watered on a regular basis, especially if you are growing in a very hot environment or one that does not receive a lot of rain.

Although you are going to be starting out with nutrient rich soil, it will have to be replaced every few years even if you are rotating your plants. One way to avoid this is to use a lot of compost in your soil after you harvest your plants as well as before you plant them. It is important that you keep your soil nutrient rich, otherwise, you will not be able to grow nutrient rich vegetables.

Cost is a huge factor when it comes to using raised beds. Basically, you are container gardening in very large containers, therefore, if money is an issue, you may not want to use raised beds. On the other hand, if your soil simply is not good enough for you to garden in, if your body simply will not let you use traditional gardening, raised beds may be best for you.

You do not have to do anything special when it comes to the design of your raised beds. You can use a simple square bed, a rectangular bed and if you want to get a bit more creative, you can use triangles or even octagons. It is all up to you and the amount of work you want to put into the garden.

There are many different types of boxes that you can build for your garden and I want to start by talking about a standard wooden box. When you begin to build your wooden boxes, you will want to, of course, gather your wood, your hammer, and nails.

Next, you want to choose the area where you will place your box, lay out 4 boards, one for each side of the box, as if you were laying the box out. This will allow you to see exactly where your box is going to be when it is completed, how much space it will take up, and allow you to decide if you want to move the box before actually building it.

The next thing you want to do is dig holes in the ground, where you will place your corner posts. Of course, you don't have to place the posts in the ground, but doing so will help make your box more secure. If you do not want to place the posts in the ground, you can place them on the ground at this point.

If your box is going to be longer than 8 feet in any direction, you will want to add center posts along the side of the board to help stabilize it. You can, of course, use any wood that you have available, but I suggest using 4x4 pieces that can be purchased at your local lumber yard (If you do not have a table saw, you can measure your area and have everything precut before bringing it home).

The next thing that you are going to do is line up one side board with your post. Using screws and a drill, or a hammer and nails, attach the sideboard to the post, lining up the edges. Continue attaching all of the sides of the bed and then you will want to place some type of barrier on the bottom of the bed.

You can use ½ inch hardware cloth that can be purchased at your local hardware store to line the bottom and sides of your box to keep the pests, animals, and weeds out of your box.

Staple the hardware cloth to the sides of the box before filling the box with soil. You can go one step further and add a layer of weed cloth if you want to ensure that absolutely no weeds get through and into your garden.

Now it is time for you to begin filling the bed with soil. You do not want the soil to be too loose so once you have placed the soil in the box and have spread it out evenly, walk across the top of the soil to pack it down, ensuring it is not loose.

If the soil is too loose, the plant's roots will not be able to take hold and as soon as you water your plants for the first time, the soil is going to become compacted and lower than you want it to be. You want the soil to be no lower than 2 inches below the top of the bed.

Now it is time to add your plants and watch them grow. Make sure that you add compost to your boxes each year after you have removed old plants and right before adding new ones. You should also rotate your plants to ensure you do not strip the soil of all of its nutrients.

Another way to create raised beds is to repurpose other items you may already have or that you can get fairly cheap. One example would be old metal file cabinet drawers. The best file cabinets that you can use to make boxes out of are the ones that are much wider than they are deep but you can use anything you want.

For this example, we will talk about an old metal file cabinet. You can usually get these fairly cheap from companies that are upgrading or going paperless or from resale shops.

Begin by choosing the area where you will be placing your boxes. The great thing about these boxes is that you can move them anywhere you want, rearranging them until you have them perfectly placed for the design of your garden.

It is important that you do not get filing cabinets that are full of rust or falling apart. They do need to be in decent condition if you want to use them in your garden.

After you have the drawers taken out of your file cabinet, you will want to remove the tracks as well, if at all possible. Next, sand down the inside of the cabinet, removing the paint if there is any.

Now you can repaint the outside of each of the drawers as well as the entire cabinet. Choose fun colors that will make your new garden stand out. However, you do need to make sure that the paint is safe to use around plants.

Once you have your boxes looking the way you want, you can place them where you want them. Some people choose to place the large file cabinet in the center of the garden and place the smaller drawer boxes around the file cabinet. However, you want to do it is completely fine as long as the design works for you.

To protect the metal from damage, you will want to line it. Weed liner is great for this purpose, but it is important to remember that the file cabinet is going to rust at some point and if you do not use a liner, it is only going to rust that much faster.

Because the file cabinet is sealed, meaning water is not going to be able to drain, you will need to use a medium such as river rock on the bottom of the bed, before adding your soil, which will allow the water to drain away from the soil. Alternatively, you can drill several holes in the bottom of your box (before placing the liner), which will allow the water to naturally drain off. If you are using a medium, you will want it to be no less than 3 inches deep.

Now it is time to add your soil. Again, you want to make sure that the soil is packed down before placing your plants. Add your plants, rotating them each year, and resupplying nutrients to the soil through compost.

Finally, you can make boxes out of bricks. Some people also choose cinder blocks, but for this example, we are going to talk about simple bricks.

Begin by gathering your bricks and taking them to the area where you want to build your box. When you are creating this box, you need to make sure you know exactly where you are going to place it because once you begin building, you are not going to want to move it.

It is important for you to think about the size and the height of your box before you purchase your garden bricks. Take some time to look at the bricks available and as stated in the first chapter, take the time to plan because you do not want to purchase more bricks than you need. Remember, it is better to have to go back and purchase more bricks than it is to have extra bricks laying around your yard.

Before you begin building the box, you need to level the ground. You want to make sure that where you plan on building your box is completely level so that your box will be level.

Next, begin laying out the box brick by brick. You want to lay out the first layer of bricks, then take a step back and make sure it is exactly what you want before moving on to the second layer. If you need to make adjustments in the length or width, this is the time to do it, not three or four layers down the road.

Once you are happy with the length and width of your box, you can begin building up the rest of the layers until you are happy with the height.

It is important for you to stagger the bricks as you are building up the box because if you simply place them one on top of the other in a perfect row, they are going to fall over if you build them up too high. Staggering means that you never line the edges of a brick up with the edges of the brick below it. You can create many different patterns and designs by staggering the bricks so have some fun and come up with a pattern that works best for you.

Once the box has been built, you will want to purchase a very thick heavy liner. This will be placed inside of the box, allowing the edges to hang over the top edges of the box. You will trim this extra liner off later after the box is completely filled.

Now you can fill your bed with the soil, ensuring that the soil is packed down well before adding your plants. Trim the edges of your liner a little at a time until you get the look you want, then add your plants.

As stated before, make sure that you rotate your plants each year and replenish the nutrients in your soil by adding compost after the harvest and before planting new plants.

Chapter 3: Choosing Your Soil, and Improving and Maintaining the Composition

The most important factor in the health of your garden is the composition of the soil. This means that to ensure you have a healthy garden, you have to have soil that contains the proper balance of minerals, air, organic material, and water.

Therefore, if you want to have a healthy garden, you have to know the composition of your soil so you can use techniques that will enhance the areas of the soil that needs to be enhanced.

If you are using traditional gardening, you are not going to be able to do much when it comes to choosing the composition of your soil, unless, of course, you are adding extra soil to your garden.

In this chapter, I want to talk to you about how you can choose the best soil composition for your garden and how you can maintain that composition so you do not have to continually replace your soil year after year.

The majority of plants will grow best if they are planted in soil that is 40% silt, 40% sand, and 20% clay. This type of soil is called loam and is the perfect balance for holding water for the roots of your plants while not allowing them to become waterlogged.

However, simply mixing 40% silt, 40% sand and 20% clay is not going to give you the perfect soil. Your soil must contain organic material, which is going to be decayed animals and plants. This is what is going to help the soil bind together and organic matter is going to help increase the nutrients in the soil.

Beetles, earthworms, and other organisms are also needed in your soil because they are going to allow air to get to the roots by creating empty spaces in the soil. As they die, they are going to add more organic material to the soil as well.

It is important for you to add organic material to your soil every year to help it remain a healthy environment for your plants to grow in.

Now, let's talk about how we can choose the best soil for our garden. After we discuss how you can choose the proper soil composition, we are going to talk about how you can make sure that the composition is maintained, ensuring that you do not have to keep replacing the soil.

The first thing you want to think about is how much you can afford. You see, if you want to have the highest quality soil quickly, you will want to purchase potting soil, but as we all know, potting soil can be very expensive, especially when compared to top soil.

For example, simply filling a 4x4 bed with potting soil, only six inches deep, is going to cost about $60. However, if you purchase top soil, it is going to be under $20.

The next thing you need to think about is what is in the soil, meaning are you worried that it could be contaminated? When you purchase top soil, you want to make sure that it is disease free, free of weeds, and free of pesticides. Most of the time, when you purchase top soil, you are not going to know where it came from or what contaminants are in it. You do not want to kill your garden with the soil you choose.

You also need to think about how long you want your soil to last. You see, once you put top soil on your garden or in your boxes, it is there pretty much until you move it. On the other hand, potting soil is made up of organic material, which means that it is going to completely decompose. Therefore, you will notice that your potting soil is going to disappear year after year until it is completely gone (usually about 3 years).

When it comes to potting soil in your garden, you need to know that chances are, you are going to lack nutrients after the first year. Some of the minerals you need are going to build up while others disappear, which will leave your nutrient levels unbalanced and cause issues with the health of your plants.

Even when you purchase top soil that is dark and feels great, it may not be balanced, which means it may not grow healthy plants. To ensure you have healthy soil, it is important to have it tested, checking the macro-nutrient levels, the organic material levels, CC, pH, and the micro-nutrients.

A lab test of your soil costs less than $15 in most states or you can choose to do a home test. A lab test is going to let you know if your soil is lacking any nutrient or if there is an excess of any nutrient, how much fertilizer you need to use in your soil, if you need to use lime or sulfur to improve the pH levels of the soil, the amount of organic material in the soil, and how you can fertilize your soil based on the CEC levels.

Don't waste your time and money on a garden if you have not had to the soil tested. So many times, I have heard people complaining about how much they have put into their garden, how hard they have worked, and they still can't understand why their plants are not healthy. Of course, when I ask them about their lab test results, they have no idea what I am talking about. It is a simple test that takes no time at all; simply send in samples to be tested or test them yourself to ensure you have the best soil for your garden.

Improving the composition is the next thing I want to talk about. After all, if your test comes back and you find out that you do not have the healthy soil you thought you did.

The first result of your lab test that you will want to look at is the pH of your soil. The pH of your soil should be neutral, which means that it has a pH of 7.0. If your test results show that the pH levels of your soil are higher than 7.0, this means your soil is alkaline. If the test results show that your pH levels of your soil are less than 7.0, it means that your soil is acidic.

Having slightly acidic soil is perfectly fine as most plants prefer a slightly acidic environment. As long as your test results range between 6.0 and 7.0, your plants will do fine. Anything out of this range means that the soil needs improving.

If the soil is too acidic, you will want to add limestone to the garden to increase the pH levels. However, if the soil is too alkaline, you will want to add sulfur to your garden to lower the pH levels of the soil and create a healthy environment for your plants to grow.

After you have the pH levels of your soil under control, you will want to focus on the amount of organic material in the soil. According scientific studies done by the University of Georgia, you want your soil to be about 5% organic material.

To add organic matter to your garden, you will want to start by choosing the organic material you wish to add. You can use leaves that have been piling up around your yard, compost, and manure. If you are using leaves, it is important for you to mix them in with the soil at least a month before you begin planting your garden to let it decompose some.

Compost is another great way to add organic material to your garden and keep it out of the trash. I am going to talk about composting in a later chapter, but this is great for adding organic material as well as vitamins and nutrients to your soil.

Finally, manure is a great option if it is available to you. Simply mixing it in with your soil is going to ensure you have the proper amount of organic material in your garden.

You will want to begin by placing at least 1 inch but no more than 2 inches of organic material on your garden. If you are just starting out, or have found that your soil is lacking in organic material through lab testing, you should go ahead and add 2 inches.

After you have added the organic material on top of the soil, you will want to work it into the ground at least 6 inches. This is not a glamorous job but has to be done if you want your plants to be healthy and produce as much as they can. The best way to do this is to work in small sections using a wheel barrel and shovel.

Place the material on a small section of the garden and then work it into the soil before moving to the next section. This will help you avoid walking through manure or compost.

If you are using compost, but purchasing it instead of using your own compost, there are a few things you need to ask. The first thing that you need to know is if the compost contains any heavy metals. These metals can get into your food and make you very sick; they can also leach out into the water and make you very sick as well.

You should also ask if the compost is safe to use in a vegetable garden. You see, there are some composts that will work fine for some flower gardens, particularly ones where you don't eat the flowers, but they are not safe to grow food in. It is very important that you know the difference.

Now it is time for you to aerate your soil. You will do this by digging down 1 foot below the top of the garden and creating a trench. Move over and dig another trench right next to the previous one, using the dirt from the second to fill the first. Continue doing this until you have dug up the entire garden and moved the soil from one area to the previous. Alternatively, you can use a plow set at the deepest depth to aerate your soil.

After you have done all of this, your soil will be ready for planting, but the fertilizing does not stop there. You will want to fertilize your garden about mid-growing season, too. However, things will have to be done a bit differently this time.

When you are fertilizing mid-season, you will want to place the fertilizer (compost or manure) along the sides of your plants around the base of the stem. This will allow the nutrients to seep into the soil and feed your plants. Do not dig into the soil while the plants are growing as it could damage the roots and kill the plants.

After you have harvested all of your plants from your garden, you will want to add another layer of compost or manure, working it into the soil, preparing it for the next growing season. This will be done once again before you begin planting with the new growing season.

Ensuring that you have the proper soil composition can take a lot of work, but when you are gathering all of the produce from your garden, you will quickly realize that it is well worth all of the work. By taking care of your soil, you can ensure that you will not have small unhealthy plants, but you will have large, vibrant plants that continue to produce all season long.

Chapter 4: Germinating, Planting, Growing, and Harvesting

Germination is the process that a plant goes through when they begin becoming a plant from a seed. This happens when the seed receives the right amount of water and is kept at the proper temperature for germination.

Basically, what happens is that the seed begins absorbing the water, which hydrates all of the nutrients inside of the seed. As this happens, the seed begins to swell, then you will see the beginning of a root coming out of the seed, which shows you that the seed is viable.

Once the root begins growing, you will see a small shoot starting, usually with the seed still on top of it. Eventually, the seed casing will fall off and you will have the beginning of your plant.

Many people do not see this process because they purchase their plants from a nursery, which is fine if you are only going to grow a few plants, but if your garden is going to be very large, this can become very expensive very quickly.

I want to start this chapter by talking about how you can start your seeds on your own in your own home, which is a much cheaper option than purchasing them at the nursery. However, it does take a bit of work and space if you are growing a very large garden.

When you start your own seeds or geminate them on your own, you will have a wider array of fruits and vegetables available to you to plant in your garden. Although it is okay to purchase all of your plants, you are going to find that there really is not much variety when it comes to the types of plants you will be able to grow. Geminating them on your own allows you to choose what you want to grow all year long.

Starting your seeds indoors instead of in your garden is also going to give them a head start, which means that they will be producing much faster than if you simply waited and started them in your garden. Don't get me wrong, I remember the days of going out and planting seeds with my grandfather but I also remember birds digging into the ground and getting the seeds. I remember half of the harvest being lost because the plants were not germinated indoors.

To start off with, you are going to start growing your seeds well before it becomes warm outside. Many people wait until it begins to warm up to start their seeds but this is unnecessary. You want to start them early so that as soon as it warms up and you are able to transplant them, they are big enough and strong enough to handle the transplant and thrive in your garden.

First, you will choose the seeds that you want to start, paying attention to the time it takes for them to grow to maturity. For example, some seeds will take 60 days whereas others will take 80 days to grow to maturity. You also want to pay attention to when these days start. You see, some plants will take 60 days to grow to maturity from germination whereas others will take 60 days from transplant.

Now it is time for you to choose your growing medium. It is not a good idea to simply go outside and dig up a bunch of dirt, hoping that your seeds are going to do well. You shouldn't even use the soil from your garden, but because the seeds are so delicate, you will want to use a starter mix.

This mix is sterile, light, and will hold the right amount of water for your seedlings. This is important because if there is too much water, then disease can take over or you will begin growing mold, which will quickly kill off your plants.

You should also be careful not to over water because the tiny roots of the seedlings can become water logged quite quickly, which will lead to root rot or drown your seedlings.

You can use a bagged starter mix for your seeds, pellets of peat, or coconut husk fibers, and you do not have to worry about the nutrients or fertilizers when it comes to your starter mix because the seed already contains all of the nutrients the seedling will need.

Next, you will want to choose what you are going to start your plants in. You can use cells, pots, or anything that will hold the starter mix. Personally, I like biodegradable starter cells because I do not have to worry about damaging the roots of the plants when transplanting. All you have to do is pop the plant with the cell still around the roots into your garden and the cell will decompose into your garden as the roots grow. I also like pellets of coconut husk and this is what we are using for our tomato plants this year. They are very simple to use, all you need to do is place the seed in them and water. There is no mess and as soon as you are ready to transplant, simply place the pellet into the ground.

Now it is time to think about lighting. First, let me tell you a little story about something that happened just a few weeks back. I always have a large number of seeds and had a friend who wanted to start a garden. I gave him tons of seeds, cells, and starter mix, and made sure he was ready to go. One day, I was on the phone with his wife, talking about the amount of seeds I needed to transplant when she informed me that none of the seeds I had given them had germinated. She told me they must have been bad seeds.

Knowing this was impossible, I talked to her about how they were planted, if they were getting enough water, and could not figure out why they were not growing. Then it occurred to me, in their small house, where were they keeping the seedlings?

I asked her and she told me in the basement. I am unsure how it did not occur to them that the plants would not grow in a dark, wet basement, but after I told them to bring the cells upstairs and place them in the window, they took off.

That is why I feel it is important to talk about light. Plants simply will not grow without the proper light and when you are germinating, they need a lot of light, however, you do not want them to get burned. Place your seedlings near windows that are facing east or west. It is possible for them to grow when they are near windows that are facing north and south, but they will not grow as well.

I recently did an experiment that proved just that. All of my plants on my west wall were thriving while the plants on the north wall were barely holding on. When I moved the north wall plants to the west wall, they began to thrive as well.

That brings us to temperature. Seeds germinate when the temperature is between 80 to 85 degrees, depending on the type of plant. Once they begin to sprout, they do not need to remain this warm and can be kept at room temperature between 60 and 70 degrees. This means that when you are geminating, if it is cold outside, you will not want to keep them in your windowsill or they will not germinate. Keeping them on a table near a window will ensure that they will stay warm enough but you also need to ensure they are getting enough light.

Purchasing lights at this point is not needed, but if you are having a hard time keeping your plants warm enough, placing them a few inches above a space heater will do the job. It only takes a few days for a seed to germinate and the space heater can be removed after they have begun to sprout.

Water is extremely important when it comes to your plants. This is because like humans, plants are mostly water and they have to have enough water to thrive. However, too much water can cause root rot, cause the plants to become waterlogged, and even cause them to drown.

When you are preparing to plant your seeds in your starter mix, you want to first ensure that the starter mix has been moistened. Once you have the seeds in the starter mix, you will want to cover them either with the plastic cover that came with your kit or a plastic sandwich bag to ensure you are keeping the humidity in.

Once the seeds have begun to sprout, you can remove the clear top or bags and begin watering them from the bottom up. You want to place the water in the bottom of their container because if you water them from the top, it can cause a fungus to grow. It can also dislodge the seedlings from the soil and damage the fragile sprouts.

The secret to proper germination is ensuring that the seeds are covered before they begin to sprout, then making sure they receive enough light and water to keep them growing until you are ready to transplant them.

Many people think germination is difficult, but it does not have to be. If you are afraid that you are not going to be successful, start with a few plants and begin experimenting with the proper environments. Soon, you will be an expert and starting your own seeds.

When your plants are ready and the temperature is right, you will want to transplant them into your garden. This will take a bit of planning ahead because you want the weather to be right to ensure your plants are able to adjust to their new environment.

You want to begin by choosing a mild, cloudy day that is calm and free from any wind or storms. It is best to transplant in the evening because your plants are going to need time to recover from the shock of being transplanted and they will have a hard time doing this if they are left in the hot midday sun.

You want to begin by moistening your garden soil. You do not want to soak the soil so that it becomes soggy but simply moisten it so that it will be easier for you to work with and easier for the plants to adjust to. If it has been very dry or very hot, water the area where you are planning on planting in the day before you transplant your seedling.

You also want to make sure that the soil your seedlings are planted in is moist as well. This will help the soil to remain together while you are transplanting. Of course, this does not matter if you are using pots that will decompose after being placed in the ground.

The next step is to dig a hole in your garden that is the same depth as the soil in your starter cells or the same depth as the soil in whatever container you have chosen to use. This applies to all plants except tomatoes. For tomatoes, you will want to dig the hole twice as deep.

If the plant is in a peat pot, simply place the pot with the plant in the garden and cover with soil. However, if you are using another container, it is time to remove the plant from the container. To do this, you will cup the seedling while turning over the container, a starter cell, for example, and allowing the seedling to slide out with the dirt around the root wad. If the seedling does not slide out easily, simply tap the sides of the container with your finger or press gently on the bottom of the container, ensuring you do not damage the roots.

Place the root ball in the hole you have prepared and cover with soil, firmly patting the soil down to ensure it is not loose. This will allow the roots to take hold in the new soil and it will help to keep the plant upright until the roots are able to establish themselves.

You will want to water the seedlings the following day, depending on the weather and keep the soil moist until the roots have been able to establish themselves in the new environment.

You should not be alarmed if your plants begin to look a bit droopy after they have been transplanted, especially if it was done on a very hot or sunny day. After about a day or two, they will begin to straighten up and look alive again.

After your plants have established themselves, you will have to take care of your garden to ensure your plants are receiving the water and nutrients they need. You will also have to ensure there are no bugs or other pests in your garden as well as take charge of removing the weeds.

The first thing you want to do is begin watering your plants in the morning before the sun is high in the sky. This is very important if you live in a very dry, hot area.

You also want to support your plants. Placing stakes for plants such as tomatoes is very important if you want them to grow and produce. They need support and you do not want your produce laying on the ground, rotting away.

Weeding your garden is one of the most important things you can do because it will ensure the weeds are not taking nutrients away from the plants and it will also ensure that the weeds do not take over the garden.

Keep an eye out for pests. Rabbits, raccoons, cats, and other animals are going to be attracted to your garden as well as bugs, worms, and caterpillars of all kinds. In the first chapter, I spoke about planting different types of herbs and flowers around and in your garden to keep these types of pests away, but you may find you still have to deal with them on occasion. Keep a sharp eye out for any small bites taken out of your leaves, and turn the leaves of your plants over regularly and check for pests. If you do find them, you will have to decide if you want to use chemicals in your garden or not.

Finally, it will come time for you to harvest the produce out of your garden. This is what you worked so hard for and you want to make sure you do it right. You will want to pick up a basket to take out to your garden with you every day. This will ensure that you are able to harvest the plants that have ripened quickly and ensuring that they do not end up rotting on the vine.

You want to be very careful when you are harvesting your produce so that you do not damage the plant and you want to harvest daily to ensure your plants are able to produce more for you. You see, ripened fruit is going to take a lot of nutrients away from the plant if left on the vine. However, if you pick them quickly, these nutrients can go to producing more for you throughout the entire harvest season.

Chapter 5: Composting and Its Uses

I have mentioned compost several times in the previous chapters and now I want to get into what composting actually is as well as the benefits and uses.

Composting is a process in which you use the natural process of decomposing to turn organic material into a very nutrient rich soil. You can use anything that was once alive to create compost, but when you are creating compost for your garden, you will want to be very careful about what you put into it.

When you are creating compost for your garden, there are a few items you will need to begin with. The first item is a large container that has a lid. Some people choose to build a compost bin out of wood while others use items as simple a large trash can or storage totes.

It does not matter what container you choose to use as long as you can seal the container after placing organic material inside.

One of the easiest ways to compost is to start with what you already have. Most of us already have fruit and vegetable peels that get thrown into the garbage every day. We have fruits and vegetables that go bad in our fridge waiting on us to eat them and although it breaks our hearts to throw them away, we know we must.

You can put all of this to good use by starting to compost. Each day, instead of throwing all of this organic material into the garbage, toss it into your compost bin instead and watch it decompose and turn into amazing healthy soil that you can use on your garden. Once you notice that the bottom layers of the organic material are beginning to turn to soil, you can add in a few handfuls of earthworms to help the organic material decompose quickly and ensure that it has all of the nutrients needed for your garden. If you do not want to wait, you can start with a few inches of manure, add in the earthworms, and then begin tossing in the organic material.

Some people choose to put grass clippings, leaves, and other material found around the yard in their compost and this is fine if you are going to use the compost to fertilize your yard, but if you are going to be putting it into a garden, you want to avoid yard clippings and leaves because chances are you are going to get seeds as well. What this means is that when you place the compost in your garden, it will be full of grass and weed seeds, making it difficult for you to keep your garden weed free.

Many people think that composting is simply too much trouble, so I want to spend a few moments talking about why you should compost. The first reason is because it is going to save you money. Yes, you can purchase compost for your garden, but it is going to cost you and you can never really be sure what exactly is in the compost.

Composting is a free way to use what you are already going to throw away to help you create a healthy garden. You are also going to find that you do not have to purchase chemical fertilizers, which is great if you are growing organically.

Unlike chemical fertilizers, when you compost and use it on your garden, you do not have to worry about the nutrients being washed away with each rain, which, again, saves you money.

Another reason many people compost is because it keeps organic material out of the landfills. Yes, the material will decompose, but why throw it in the landfill when your garden can benefit so much from it?

Compost helps to hold water, which means that you will have to water less often and your plants will never be without the water they must have to thrive. If you do not put compost in your garden soil, chances are, it is going to look dusty, light in color, and unhealthy. It is also going to be very dry, which means you will have to spend more time watering your garden. If you live in a very dry area, this could mean that you have to spend a lot of time watering your garden.

40% of the waste we throw away every day is compostable. Imagine what a difference it would make if everyone used that waste to create compost instead of throwing it into the landfills. This is also an important figure to know when you think about the amount of compost you can create before the planting season arrives. Just think, almost half of what you are currently throwing away could be put to good use in your garden.

What is even better news is that when your garden is done growing and you have harvested all of the produce, you can simply pluck up those plants, toss them into the compost bin and they will become part of your garden the following year!

Another great benefit of using compost is that you are going to significantly affect the amount of pests in your garden by using compost. This will reduce your need for having to use pesticides, which is what we all want when we are growing a garden.

The compost is also going to feed the beneficial organisms that you want in your garden. These organisms not only help to ensure the health of your garden, but also help to keep pests away.

Finally, by using compost on your garden, you are going to ensure that your soil has the nutrients it needs, which means your fruits and vegetables will be full of vitamins and minerals you need. Studies have shown that when fruits and vegetables are grown in soil that has been depleted of its nutrients, the plants have very low nutritional value.

You can use compost in your garden, on your lawn, and even in your flower beds so you don't have to ever worry about having too much compost to use. It can be used to start your seeds and you can even create compost tea to water your plants with.

Composting is so easy, why not give it a try? Imagine how healthy and vibrant your garden can be and how much you can save.

Chapter 6: Organic Growing

I have talked a lot about how different aspects will benefit you if you are planning on growing organically and I feel that it is important that we spend a bit of time talking about organic growing, what it is, and how you can do it.

Organic growing is a technique of growing that uses no genetically modified seeds, no chemical pesticides, and no synthetic fertilizers. In short, it is getting back to basics and growing the way it used to be done when small farms were more popular.

We have all seen the effects of using chemicals on our foods. People are becoming sick, they are lacking in nutrients even though they are eating all of the fruits and vegetables they are supposed to, they are suffering from disease, cancer is everywhere, and people are dying at a very early age.

The sad thing is that even though it is known that herbicides, pesticides, and fertilizers have been proven to cause breast cancer, birth defects, brain damage, lymphoma, Parkinson's, prostate cancer, miscarriages, leukemia, infertility, depression, autism, and many other diseases, they are still being used by big commercial farms.

This means that one of the biggest benefits of organic growing is simply the fact that you will be healthy. Not only that, but have you looked at the prices of organically grown food lately? It is nearly double that of commercially grown produce.

The reason for this is simple. It is tough. I am not going to tell you that growing organically is easy, the prices are steeper not because organic farmers think they deserve more, but because a lot more work is put into growing organically.

You see, those who grow organically are not able to run to the garden shed, pull out a spray bottle full of chemicals, and fix whatever problem comes along in their garden. They have to be very observant and understand how they can change their system to correct a problem in their garden before it destroys the entire garden.

Organic growing is more labor intensive as well. You see, as I just stated, when weeds start to pop up in the garden, they can't run and get the spray bottle, they have to get down on their hands and knees and pull each weed by the root.

So, of course, anyone could produce more crops by using non-organic methods than by growing organically. This often makes people wonder why gardeners want to grow organically.

I have already mentioned a few of the reasons, health, nutrition, and avoiding poisonous chemicals, but there are even more reasons. One huge reason people choose to grow organically is the taste of the crop. The truth is, the food you are purchasing at the grocery store that is not organically grown tastes nothing like the food you can grow organically in your garden. You really have not tasted a tomato unless you have tasted an organic tomato and that is true for all of the crops you will plant.

Because organic foods are grown naturally, they have a much longer shelf life than the produce you would purchase at your local grocery store. You see, because they are full of nutrients and are naturally grown, they do not mold and rot quickly like the produce you purchase at the store.

Another benefit, one that you will see as the grower, is that you are going to have less pests. If you follow the directions I gave you in the first chapter, planting herbs and flowers in and around your garden, you will find that you do not have to deal with pests. Most of the time, if you do get bugs, they are going to eat the unhealthy or sick plants while leaving the healthy ones alone.

Weeds are another issue many gardeners deal with, but not those who grow organically. You see, the weeds are like a Band-Aid for the soil. They grow where the nutrients have been depleted, they are there to heal the soil. However, when you take care of the soil through organic means such as composting, you will not have to worry about having a lot of weeds in your garden because the soil does not need healing.

When you garden organically, you will save a ton of money on pesticides, insecticides, and synthetic fertilizers because you simply cannot put them on organic food. If you follow the information you were given about soil composition as well as planning and planting your garden, you will have no need for any of these chemicals anyway.

The truth is, most small, family gardens are organic, however, some do still use chemicals, which just seems silly when you think about it. If you are going to take the time to grow a garden, if you are going to work hard to ensure you are growing healthy food for your family, why would you want to coat it in poison?

What is required when growing organically?

According to the USDA, to grow organically, you must not use synthetic pesticides, herbicides, or fertilizers.

This means that none of these chemicals can be used at any point during the growing process, from starting your seed to harvesting your crop. You must also use seeds that have not been genetically modified. GMO's are becoming more and more popular and can be purchased almost anywhere that sells seeds without knowing.

If you follow the information that you have learned in this book, if you use compost or manure, if you start your own seeds and know exactly how they were grown from start to finish, you will have no problem growing organically.

Many people think that those who grow organically are wasting their time, they have been lead to believe that all of those chemicals and poisons will not harm them or their families but sadly, they are mistaken. Growing organically is simply growing the way plants have always grown, growing the way our great grandparents grew, long before all of these chemicals and poisons were available to spray on the food you would be putting in your body.

It is amazing how many people forget that poison is poison, even if the USDA has approved it to be sprayed on our food. Personally, I think organic growing is best and I am sure that has been made clear in this chapter, but I also understand that every person has to make that decision for themselves. However, if you have any interest in organic growing, give it a shot and see just what it feels like to know the food you are putting on your family's plate is without all of the poison and chemicals.

Chapter 7: Water and Irrigation

We all know that without water, your garden simply will not grow so I want to take a little bit of time and talk about water in this chapter. We will also talk about irrigation later on and how you can ensure your plants are getting the amount of water they really need.

When it comes to watering, there is no exact science, but there are tips and tricks that you can learn to help you know when your plants need watered and how much they need. You will want to begin by paying attention to the soil. You do not want your soil to remain wet at all times. This means that if you go out to water your garden and the soil is already moist, they do not need any water that day.

Think about it like this, you would not water your plants right after it rained because you would know that the plants did not need the water. In the same way, you will want to learn what your soil looks like when it has been watered as well as what it feels like.

If you are container gardening, you will learn how heavy your containers will be when they need water as well as how heavy they are when they do not need water. Of course, all of this is going to take some time and I want to help you ensure you are not over watering or under watering right now.

A good rule of thumb is to water your garden 1 inch of water per week plus an extra ½ an inch of water for every 10 degrees the temperature rises over 70. However, you want to take the median of the high and the low to figure out how much water to give your plants. This means that if the high is 100 and the low is 75, you will want to give your plants 1 extra inch of water that week. Of course, you are going to have a lot more numbers than just two, but this gives you an idea of how it works. One inch of water (if you have no way to measure) is about 60 gallons of water per 100 square feet. This amount of water also includes rain water so do not over water your garden.

I already talked several times about the time of day that you should water your garden, but just to reiterate, you need to water your garden in the morning time so that it has time to dry out a bit before the cooler night temperatures. This is to ensure that you do not invite parasites, pests, or disease into your garden.

Irrigation is the method in which water is going to be supplied to your plants. If you have a small garden, a simple sprinkler will do the trick. Some people with large gardens choose to place several sprinklers in their garden, but you should understand that the more sprinklers you use, the less pressure there is going to be, which means the plants furthest from the sprinkler are going to get less water.

Many people still choose to go outside and water their garden, spraying it by hand. They find that it is a relaxing way to start their day and helps them to get their mind focused.

You can also use furrows, which are small trenches that are dug between raised beds which allow the water to go directly to the roots of the plants. When it is time to water, you will fill the furrows with water, wait a few moments, and then check to ensure the water has been absorbed. Of course, this is not the most effective way to water your garden because the plants at the beginning of the furrows are always going to receive more water than the plants at the end of the furrows.

The best way I have found to water a garden is to place small holes in a hose and string it through the garden. As you turn on the water, the hose will work as a sprinkler. This system is called soaker hose irrigation and works well because it allows you to place the hose exactly where you will need it. This is a great method to use because it literally takes no time. All you have to do is turn your pump on in the morning while you are getting ready for work and turn it off before you leave. This will ensure that your garden is getting the water it needs without taking a lot of your time.

If you use the soaker hose system, do not be concerned if there is not enough pressure to spray the foliage of your plant, as long as the ground is getting enough water, your plants will be perfectly fine.

I do suggest that if you are using an irrigation system that does not get the foliage wet, that you do water your plants by hand via a water hose once a week because you want to keep the dust off of the leaves.

Choosing your irrigation system does not have to be complicated and you do not have to go out and purchase some expensive system. All you need to do is choose a system that works for you and your garden. There is no wrong or right way when it comes to irrigation. As long as the garden is getting the water it needs and you are watering in the morning, your garden is going to grow perfectly.

When it comes to irrigation, there are many other systems you can use and many people have created their own according to their needs as well as the needs of their garden so do not feel as if you are confined to using the systems that I have talked about in this chapter.

Remember, when you water your garden properly, you are going to ensure that they are growing properly and producing the crop that you want them to produce. Watering your garden properly is going to save you time and money. It is going to save your plants from disease and it is going to ensure you have large, healthy fruit and vegetables. However, you do not want to over water your plants. Remember, you do not have to water daily. Check your soil each day before watering and don't water if the soil is already moist. Doing so will only drown your plants, cause root rot, or cause the roots to become water logged.

Chapter 8: Pest and Disease Control

Of course, we all know we can use chemicals to keep pests out of our gardens, but what if we want to grow organically or simply don't want to spray our gardens with a bunch of chemicals?

The good news is that there plenty of natural ways to control pests in your garden and I want to start this chapter by talking about those types of pest control. One of the greatest things I have learned while gardening is that no matter what the pest is, you can find a way to control it naturally and without chemicals.

However, before we get into controlling pests that have gotten into your garden, I want to talk a little bit about prevention. The easiest way to control pests in your garden is to ensure they do not come into your garden in the first place.

To do this, you will want to make sure that you are pulling out any weak plants. The plants may already have become a target for pests, but leaving them in your garden is only going to attract more pests. Pull the plant out of your garden and make sure that you dispose of it away from the garden to ensure it does not attract other pests.

As I already discussed in the previous chapter, having healthy soil is going to help prevent pests from attacking your garden. Use your compost and top off the garden with mulch after the plants have stabilized in their environment after transplanting to grow strong plants. Strong plants will not attract pests.

If you are having a hard time keeping slugs away from your garden, add some seaweed fertilizer into your mulch or spray the mulch with seaweed fertilizer. This will help the plants grow stronger, help them fight disease, and keep the slugs away.

Keep any debris, weeds, and leaves away from the garden to minimize the chances of bugs taking up residence near your garden. You should also keep your mulch free from weeds and leaves to avoid attracting bugs.

Rotate your crops each year to keep the bugs away. Most insects will only focus on one type of plant. To ensure that your plants do not become infested, rotate them every year. This will also help to ensure your soil does not become depleted of vital nutrients.

Plant herbs around specific plants that you know are prone to infestation. I have already provided you with a list of herbs and how you can use them in your garden to prevent insects from attacking your crops and if you are not using chemicals, I highly suggest adding the herbs in between your other plants.

There are beneficial insects that you do want in your garden so before we move on, I want to cover a few of these just to ensure you do not end up killing them off.

Lady bugs will kill aphids, mites, scale, and white flies, which can destroy your garden. To attract ladybugs to your garden, plant daisies around it. You can also purchase ladybugs online and place them in your garden.

Ichneumon wasps will eat caterpillars that cause damage to the leaves of your plants. To attract them, you can plant carrots, parsley, and celery.

Lacewings will eat aphids as well as their larva and many other pests. They are attracted to yarrow and asters. They can also be purchased online and placed in your garden.

Hover flies are going to eat aphids as well other pests; they are also attracted to yarrow and goldenrod.

Praying mantis will eat most garden pests and the eggs can be purchased online. It does not take long for a praying mantis to reach maturity, so place the eggs in your garden and before you know it, the praying mantis will be protecting your fruits and veggies.

Nematodes are very effective when it comes to keeping cutworms out of your garden. They also keep beetles out as well as many other pests. The eggs are very small and come in a sponge containing a million. Once you mix them with water, you will place them on the soil and wait for them to hatch. Nematodes are not harmful to pets or people and can be purchased at most garden centers.

Now that you know how to prevent the pests from getting into your garden, let's talk about a few non-toxic remedies just in case your garden does fall victim.

For most insects, you will mix a few drops of Natural Ivory soap into one quart of water with 1 tablespoon of canola oil. Shake the mixture well and place it into a spray bottle. Spray directly on the plant from the top down, then spray the underside of the leaves from the bottom up. The oil will smother the insects, but will not harm your plant.

Now it is time to talk about disease. Chances are, disease control is going to be your biggest issue when it comes to growing, especially if you live in a hot, humid environment. This is because this is the perfect environment for disease to thrive on when it comes to your garden.

You will find that fungus will grow on living plants as well as plants that have already died. The moist, hot environment of the garden is perfect for fungus to grow in and it can be the most difficult issue you have to face.

Bacteria also reproduce very quickly in warm environments, which means that if one of your plants becomes infected with bacteria, it can spread quickly throughout your entire garden if it is not quickly handled.

Viruses are spread through insects and will infect a plant's cells before multiplying and eventually being spread on to a new plant via an insect.

Again, before we talk about treating disease, I want to talk about preventing them because prevention truly is the best medicine. Once again, it comes down to having healthy soil. You want to ensure that you are providing your plants with the best soil possible, ensuring that they are strong enough to fight off disease on their own.

Soil building is going to be something that you focus on the entire time you are gardening and because so much of your garden depends on the soil, you want to make sure that it is the best, healthiest, and nutrient rich soil possible.

Ensure that there is adequate space between your plants, allowing plenty of air flow. One of the reasons many people see disease spread so quickly in their gardens is because of overpopulation. Just like over population in the human race often leads to the spread of disease, it is the same when it comes to your garden. Diseases love hot, stagnant air, which means that if you are ensuring proper airflow in your garden, you will not have to worry about diseases spreading.

You also want to have good sanitation habits. These are very important when gardening, but even more so when you are growing food you are going to eat. Keep all lawn debris away from your garden; this includes grass clippings, sticks and leaves. You should also remove any dying plants from the garden as well as remove dying leaves from your plants. Dispose of any diseased plants away from your garden as well as away from your compost bin because these plants can cause disease in the years to come.

If you are purchasing your plants, you want to inspect them thoroughly before bringing them home and keep them in quarantine away from your other plants for several days until you are positive they are not sick or carriers of any disease.

Do not water your plants in the evening because it is going to provide diseases with a cold, damp place to thrive in. Instead, as I have stated, due to many other issues throughout this book, make sure that you water early in the morning so that your garden is dry by the time night comes.

Now it comes to treating a plant that is already infected with a disease. If you are dealing with a fungal infection, apple cider vinegar is the answer. Seaweed spray is going to help fight off diseases as well and 3% hydrogen peroxide can be sprayed directly on leaves to prevent and treat bacterial infections. Although it will not harm your plants, it should not be used on seedlings.

Treating disease in your garden can be a lot of work and a pain. It can take a lot of time and you will not be able to save all of your plants. However, preventing the disease is much easier and is going to save you a ton of time down the road. Take the steps before planting to prevent disease and you will reap the benefits in the future.

Chapter 9: Season Extension

A season extension is anything that is going to allow you to continue to harvest your crop after the regular growing season has ended. Of course, we would all love to continue to harvest our crops after the growing season has ended and that is what I want to focus on in this chapter.

There are two basic principles to season extension and they are to protect the plants from frost as well as ensuring the plants do not become overheated. This is done to speed the growth of the plants and ensure that the plants produce in higher quantity with higher quality.

The techniques used for season extension vary greatly when it comes to their difficulty, which means that they can range from very simple to extremely complicated and labor intensive.

One of the simplest techniques is early maturing. This means that you start your seedlings early and get them to maturity before most people are beginning to plant. This will allow you to begin harvesting quickly and will allow you to harvest more crops from your plant during the growing season.

A more complex technique would involve using plastic mulch to start growing your plants early on, before the soil is normally warm enough to grow in.

Of course, using any technique to extend your growing season can come with a downside and I will cover those as we work through this chapter.

Here are a few examples of season extension techniques:

1. Raised beds. We talked about raised beds earlier in this book, but they are used as a season extension technique because the soil in the beds heats up

much faster than the soil on the ground, which, of course, allows for earlier planting. If this is used with early maturing, you can end up seeing crops very quickly.

2. Mulches are also used as a season extension technique. Mulch is any material that you place around the plant on top of the soil in your garden. When it comes to season extension techniques, plastic mulches are often used and are nothing more than a sheet of plastic that has been placed on the ground. Slits are cut through the plastic, which allows the plant to grow. This type of mulch is great for reducing the amount of weeds in your garden, keeping the soil moist, increasing the temperatures of the soil, which means earlier planting as well as later harvests and they help to speed up the growth of the plant, too. If you are growing organically, plastic mulches are permitted, however, the plastic must be removed from the garden at the end of each growing season.

3. Row covers are small fabrics that are light and porous. They are used to place over the plant, which allows the plant to retain heat. This means the plant is able to be protected when it is still frosting outside and they also provide protection from insects.

4. Cold frames are a small enclosure that is built low to the ground and has a clear roof. It is used to protect the plants from frost and cold weather. You can purchase these frames at garden centers and they are often used for seedlings that are still in their starter cell and are to be transplanted later.

5. High tunnels function much like a greenhouse in that they are metal frames that have been covered in clear plastic sheeting. The down side is that they

are generally not hot enough to extend the season very long, however, they are created so that they can be moved around, which is great when it comes to rotating your crops.

6. A greenhouse is, of course, a great technique when it comes to season extension because it will allow your crops to grow all year, even when the temperatures drop below zero outside.

There are several advantages to season extension, including higher productivity, higher yields, and better quality. For those who are growing for profit, this means a higher income and a gain in customers.

Even though these are great advantages, there are also some disadvantages, including no break between growing seasons and increased risk of crop failure; and if you are gardening for a profit, it can lead to higher production costs.

If you are gardening for a profit, it can be to your advantage to use season extension techniques. However, if you are gardening simply to feed your family, it is unnecessary and can be more trouble than it is worth.

Chapter 10: Maximizing Use of Small Spaces

To finish up this book, I want to talk about how you can make the most of your small garden space. I am going to give you the best tips and tricks to ensure you can make the most of your space because after all, it does not matter how little space you have, everyone deserves a thriving garden.

1. Grow food instead of grass. Of course, if you have children, you will want a space in your yard for them to play, but look around your yard and think about all of the space that is just being used to grow grass. Imagine how your yard would look with a nice blueberry bush growing in it, or how easy it would be to grow beans up the trellis. Do you want to plant trees in your yard? How about a nice fruit tree instead of a simple oak? Get creative when you are looking around your yard and imagine all that you can grow. Remember, a garden doesn't have to be rows of plants in a rectangle, use the space you have in a way that works with your lifestyle.

2. Look at the space you have on your balcony as well. Don't forget the space up above. Remember when the Topsy turvy came out years ago and everyone was growing tomatoes from their balcony? Well, guess what? It still works and it is a great way to make use of your space. You can use containers to grow on your balcony, too. Lettuce, herbs, and many other short plants, even peppers and tomatoes, do great in containers.

3. Take advantage of companion planting. These come from the Native American technique called the three sisters, where three plants are grown in the

47

same area and they benefit from each other. For example, corn, beans, and squash. The corn grows and creates a 'pole' for the beans to climb as they grow, the beans are going to ensure that the corn and squash have enough nitrate and the squash is going to keep any weeds from growing.

4. Take advantage of indoor space, too. In my house, you can guarantee that if you open any curtain, there is going to be an herb garden in the window sill. Not only will doing this provide you with healthy, fresh herbs to cook with, but it also helps provide fresh air in your home.

5. Grow vertically. Instead of allowing your vegetables to grow out, taking up precious space on the ground, train them to grow up. If you use this technique throughout your garden, it can save you a ton of space and allow you to grow much more than you thought possible.

6. Use window boxes to plant salad mix. Planting all of your favorite lettuces and spinach in a window box is a great way to save space and to keep your favorite salad mix off of the ground and away from bugs and other critters such as rabbits.

7. Don't worry about planting in rows. Of course, cute rows of vegetables look nice, but what about all of that lost space? Place smaller plants of different varieties in between your plants to maximize the space you do have.

8. Plant only what you will eat. Many gardeners go to extremes when they begin planting. They plant every seed they can get their hands on, never taking the time to consider if they or anyone in their family will eat the vegetable. Often times, this means that space is wasted and so is the crop. One example of this is pumpkins. It seems that no matter where I

go, everyone has pumpkins in their garden. When I ask them if they eat them, the answer is no, they are for Halloween. Having one or two pumpkin plants for your children is fine, but trying to create a pumpkin patch when you have limited space is just wasting space you could use for something you will actually benefit from.

9. Don't plant vegetables that you can purchase cheap all year round. One example of this is organic carrots. Where I live, it is not necessary for me to plant carrots because they are only 99 cents a bag year round. Planting the amount of carrots that we eat would mean I have to use half of my garden to do so and it would waste a lot of space I could use for other more expensive vegetables.

10. Plant outside of your garden. Instead of worrying about that flower garden, why not plant some strawberries? It is much better for you to use the space you do have for food instead of flowers. Of course, you can use fruits and vegetable plants to make your yard look just as beautiful if you place them strategically.

Making the most out of the space you have does take a bit of creativity, but I hope that with these 10 tips, you have begun to get some ideas. The best way for you to decide how you will make the most of the space you have is to take a walk around your yard. Look at all of the extra space that is being used for nothing and figure out a way to maximize it. If there is no space on the ground, start looking up. Remember that there is always more space than what we think there is and if you use it right, you can have an abundance of fruits and vegetables in no time flat.

One final note, you do not have to have a lot of space to have a huge harvest. Unless you are selling your produce, you can grow what is needed in very small spaces so you should never feel that you don't have enough space to grow what you love. Be picky about what you do grow, you don't want to grow cabbage in a small garden because they need about 1 square foot per plant. However, growing them around the edge of your house is a great way to add some character and make use of the space you do have.

Conclusion

I hope this book was able to help turn you into a gardening pro. The initial stages and learning curve can be very difficult and you may end up with yields slightly smaller than you want in the beginning, but I promise that if you stick with it, you will, without a doubt, have a thriving garden full of fruits and vegetables. Nothing is better than walking outside to your garden and plucking off some fresh produce to eat. Not only are you saving money by growing them yourself, but you also have the ability to control the quality of your food, thus leading you to healthier living.

Because you have finished reading this book, the next step is to plan your garden, choose your soil and nutrients, and start earning your green thumb! With time and practice, you will have more produce than you know what to do with!

Finally, if you enjoyed this book, would you be kind enough to leave a review? It would be greatly appreciated!

Thanks again,

Charlie Tucker

www.ingramcontent.com/pod-product-compliance
Lightning Source LLC
Chambersburg PA
CBHW060616030426
42337CB00018B/3079